Tips & Hints

Terms:

ADD BEADS - Always thread beads onto filler cords unless otherwise instructed.

FOLD CORD IN HALF - Find the center and fold the cord in half.

KNOTTING CORDS - Longer cords are used to tie knots.

FILLER CORDS - Shorter cords are used for fillers, which you will knot around. Beads will usually be strung on these cords.

Basic Tips:

TIGHTENING KNOTS - For a strong ending knot, tighten each cord individually. If possible, use pliers to pull cords tight.

RUNNING OUT OF CORD - Sometimes you can switch the remaining filler cord with the knotting cord and get a few more knots. Switching cords will show, so hide change in a bead or in the middle of a knot if possible.

TACKY GLUE - Use tacky glue to secure knots and ends.

How to Measure:

Knotting cords should be 5 to 6 times as long as the finished piece if you are using closely knotted Square Knots or Half Knot Twists. The more spaces or beads, the shorter the knotting cords can be. If you knot tightly, you will need more cord. If your knots tend to be loose, you will not use as much cord. It's always better to have too much, rather than not enough!

Tools:

Cut hemp with sharp scissors.

Optional: Small pliers for tightening knots.

Happy Endings:

Begin each project with an Overhand Knot, leaving a loop. End with one or two Overhand Knots. Slip this knot through the beginning loop.

Closure

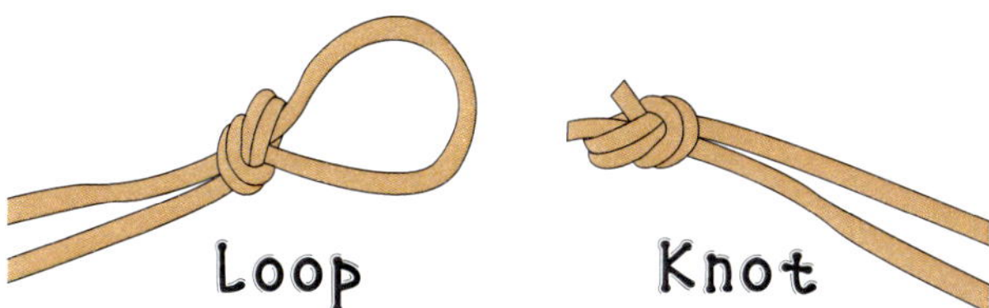

KNOTS

Finishing

LOOP and KNOT CLOSURE (page 3) - The standard loop and knot closure does not require any additional purchase.

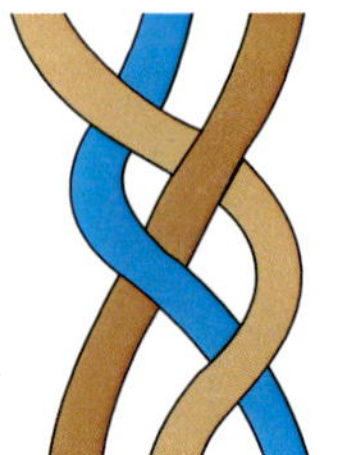

It is a good idea to leave about ¼" between the end of the piece and the final knot. This gives the loop a place to lie and makes a more secure closure.

TIP: Braid the cords before tying the Overhand Knot at the beginning for a cleaner look or braid the cords at the end of the knotting patterns before tying the final Overhand Knots.

CLASP CLOSURE - Some people prefer a metal jewelry clasp to hook the project in place.

Length of Projects

You can always make your project shorter or longer. Add beads or knots to make it longer. To make it shorter, tie fewer knots at the ends, or place fewer beads in the center.

The more beads you add to a project the fewer knots you will need and the shorter your knotting cord can be.

You must cut the cords longer to make the project longer.

TIP: Remember, it is **always better** to have too much cord than not enough!

Meanings of Bead Colors

RED – Love, passion, energy, enthusiasm, courage

ORANGE – Strength, authority, attraction, joy, success

YELLOW – Clairvoyance, learning, mind, communication

GREEN – Healing, money, prosperity, luck, fertility

BLUE – Meditation, healing, tranquility, forgiveness

PURPLE – Spirituality, wisdom, psychic awareness

WHITE – Protection, peace, purity, truth

PINK – Emotional love, friendship, affection, harmony

SEA GREEN – Calming, emotional healing, protection

ROSE – Self love, enhancing relationships

BLACK – Absorption and destruction of negative energy

LAVENDER – Intuition, dignity, spiritual shield

PEACH – Gentle strength, joy

TURQUOISE – Awareness, meditation, creativity

Basic 'Beady Buddy' Assembly

Instructions

1. Fold the head/body/leg cord in half, tie an Overhand Knot leaving a loop for hanging.

2. Add head bead and body bead to cords. Do not push together.

3. Separate the two cords. Add leg beads to each cord. Tie off loosely.

4. Thread an arm cord through the body cords.

5. Add arm beads to both ends of the arm cord, tie off.

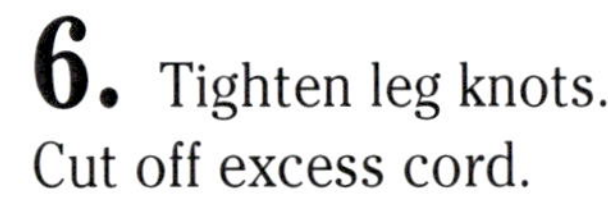

6. Tighten leg knots. Cut off excess cord.

Hemp Beady Buddies

There's a Beady Buddy for Every Buddy!

Use the same basic pattern to create 'Beady Buddies' with different color beads.

Materials for Hemp 'Beady Buddies'

LARGE BUDDIES:
• 14" piece of 1mm Natural hemp for head, body and leg cord
• 7" piece of 1mm Natural hemp for arm cord
• Large bead for body
• Smaller bead for head
• 2 to 12 beads as needed for arms and legs

MEDIUM BUDDIES:
• 12" piece of 1mm Natural hemp for head, body and leg cord
• 7" piece of 1mm Natural hemp for arm cord
• Medium bead for body
• Smaller bead for head
• 2 to 12 beads as needed for arms and legs

SMALL BUDDIES:
• 10" piece of 1mm Natural hemp for head, body and leg cord
• 5" piece of 1mm Natural hemp for arm cord
• Small bead for body
• Smaller bead for head
• 2 to 12 small beads for arms and legs

Use different beads to create a variety of sizes and shapes of bead dolls with hemp cord. Make and trade a 'Beady Buddy' with every friend.

Overhand Knot

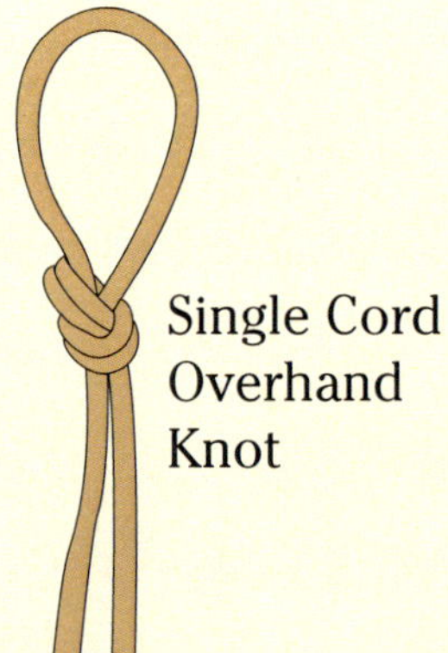

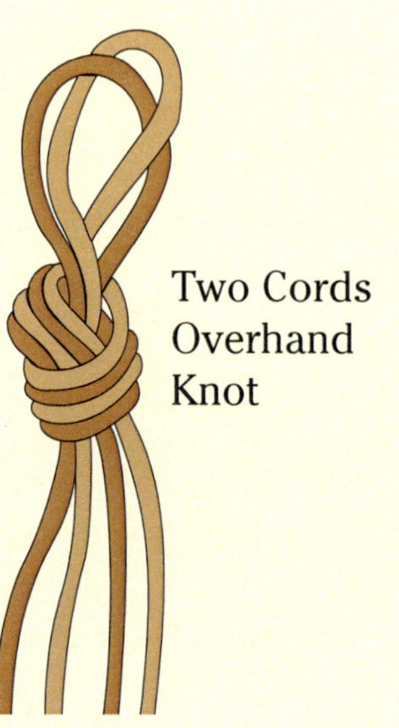

The Overhand Knot is the basic knot to begin almost any project. It creates a loop for hanging a Beady Buddy and it can be used as part of the knot & loop closure.

Basic Overhand Knot

Single Cord Overhand Knot

Two Cords Overhand Knot

Red Horn Bead Bracelet

MATERIALS:
- 65" piece of 1mm Natural hemp
- Twenty-four 8mm Red horn disc beads

1. Fold the cord 14" from one end, tie an Overhand Knot, leaving a ½" loop. Use the long end as a knotting cord, use the short end as a filler/bead carrier cord.

2. Tie Half Hitch Twists for 1". Add a bead to the filler cord, tie one Half Hitch Twist Knot. Continue to add one bead, tie one Half Hitch Twist until all beads have been added. Tie Half Hitch Twists for 1". Tie 2 Overhand Knots, one on top of the other. Trim the ends.

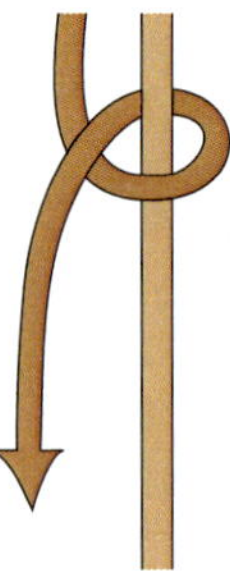

Half Hitch Twist see page 8

Brass Bell Anklet

MATERIALS:
- 36" piece of 1mm Natural hemp
- 12 small brass bells
- Twenty-four ¾" tube horn beads

1. Fold the cord 5" from one end, tie an Overhand Knot leaving a ½" loop. Dot the knot with glue, tie another Overhand Knot on top of the first knot, pull it very tight. Trim the short end.

2. Add Beads: one tube bead, one brass bell, one tube bead. Tie 2 Overhand Knots, one on top of the other. Continue to add beads and bells in this manner until all have been added.

3. Leave a ¼" space after the last Overhand Knot. Tie 2 or 3 Overhand Knots on top of each other. Trim the end.

Bracelets & Anklets

Blue Bead Bracelet

MATERIALS:
- One 25" piece of 1mm Natural hemp
- Thirty-nine ¼" Blue glass donuts

1. Fold the cord in half. Tie an Overhand Knot, leaving a ½" loop.

2. Add 3 donut beads. Tie two Overhand Knots, one on top of the other.

3. Repeat Step 2 five times; add the 'Beady Buddy'. Repeat Step 2 six times. Tie four Overhand Knots, one of top of the other. Trim the ends.

'Beady Buddy' Materials:

- One ¼" Ivory bead
- One ½" Chevron bead
- Twelve ¼" Blue donut beads
- One 6" piece 1mm Natural hemp for body
- One 5" piece 1mm Natural hemp for arms

Follow 'Beady Buddy' Instructions on pages 4-5.

Wear and Share these darling 'Beady Buddy' bracelets and dolls.

Yellow Striped Bead Bracelet

MATERIALS:
- One 22" piece of 2mm Natural hemp
- Eight ½" tube horn beads

1. Fold cord 5" from one end, tie Overhand Knot leaving ½" loop. Dot with glue, pull knot very tightly. Trim short end.

2. Add bead, tie Overhand Knot. Repeat until all beads have been added.

3. Leave ¼" space after last Overhand Knot, tie Overhand Knot. Tie second Overhand Knot over first knot. Trim end.

Horn Tube Necklace

MATERIALS:
- 120" piece of 1mm Natural hemp for knotting cord
- 88" piece of 1mm hemp for filler cords
- Six 1" faceted horn tube beads
- Twelve ¼" Black glass donut beads

1. Fold the 120" piece of cord at a point 22" from one end. Fold filler cord in half, put folds together. Tie an Overhand Knot, leaving a ½" loop. Tie **Half Hitch** Twist for 3½", using the long cord as knotting cord.

2. Add one donut bead, one tube bead and one donut bead to all cords. Tie Half Hitch Twist for ½". Repeat until all beads have been added.

3. Tie Half Hitch Twist for 3½". Tie 2 Overhand Knots, one on top of the other. Trim the ends.

Black Trade Bead Necklace

MATERIALS:
- 140" piece of 1mm Natural hemp for knotting cord
- 45" piece of 1mm hemp for filler cord
- 1½" Black trade bead
- Thirty-six ¼" Red glass donut beads

1. Fold cords in half, tie an Overhand Knot leaving a ½" loop. Tie **Half Knot** Twist for 2".

2. Add 3 donut beads, tie Half Knot Twist for ¾". Repeat 6 times.

3. Add a large Black bead, tie Half Knot Twist for ¾". Repeat Step 2 six times. Tie Half Knot Twist for 2". Tie 2 Overhand Knots, one on top of the other. Trim the ends.

Blue Bead Choker

MATERIALS:
- Three 80" pieces of 1mm Natural hemp
- Nine ¼" Blue White Heart beads

1. Fold cords in half, tie Overhand Knot leaving ½" loop. Tie 4-Strand Alternating Square Knot pattern for 5".

2. Pin aside one knotting cord. With 3 cords, tie 3 Square Knots over one filler cord. Add bead to other cord. Tie one Square Knot with all 4 cords. Repeat this step until all 9 beads have been added.

3. Tie 4-Strand Alternating Square Knot pattern for 5". Tie Overhand Knot with all cords. Tie another Overhand Knot on top of first knot. Trim ends.

4-Strand Alternating Knot

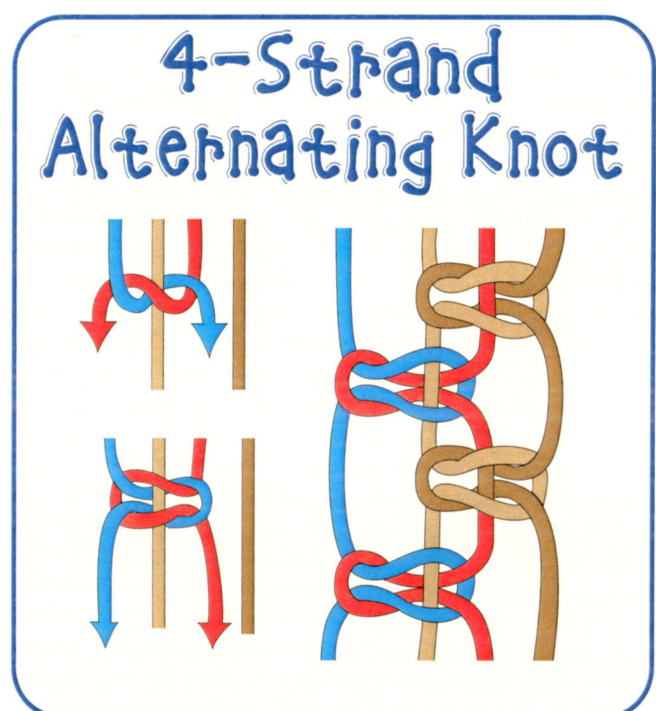

Red & Blue Bead Twist Choker

MATERIALS:
- 115" piece of 1mm Natural hemp for knotting cords
- 38" piece of 1mm hemp for filler cords
- Eight 8mm round horn beads
- Twelve ¼" Blue glass donut beads

1. Fold both cords in half. Tie an Overhand Knot with both cords, leaving a ½" loop. Tie 8 Square Knots. Tie **Half Knot** Twist for 2".

2. Add one donut bead, one horn bead, one donut bead to all cords. Tie Half Knot Twist for ¾". Repeat this step until all beads have been added.

3. Tie Half Knot Twist for 2". Tie 8 Square Knots. Tie 2 Overhand Knots, one on top of the other. Trim the ends.

Brass Bell Wind Chime

Brass Bell Wind Chime

MATERIALS:
- Six 66" pieces of 1mm Natural hemp
- Two 3-hole bone spacer bars
- Three 1¾" horn hair pipe beads
- Six 7mm Patina brass beads
- 6 small brass bells

1. Fold all the cords in half. Tie an Overhand Knot with all the cords, leaving a 1" loop for hanging. Separate the cords into 3 groups of 4 cords. Tie **Half Knot** Twist for 1½" with each group.

2. Thread each group of cords through a hole in a spacer bar.

3. Add 1 brass patina bead, 1 horn bead, 1 brass bead on each group of cords.

4. Thread each group of cords through a hole in a second spacer bar.

5. Tie Half Knot Twist for 1". Tie an Overhand Knot with each group of cords.

6. Add a bell to one pair of cords from a group, position the bell about 4" down the cord. Fold cords up and tie an Overhand Knot, leaving a small loop at the end with the bell hanging freely in the loop. Pull knots snug. Trim the ends. Repeat with each pair of cords.

Create a decorative wind chime for outside... or in!

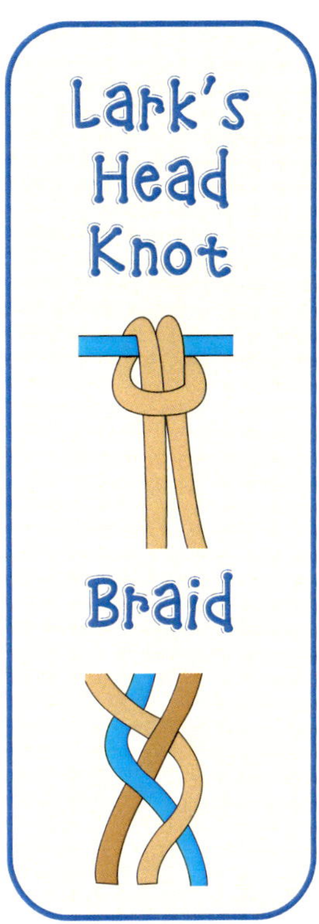

Watch Band

Hemp and Beads Watchband

MATERIALS:
- Four 72" pieces of 1mm Natural hemp
- Three 6" pieces of 1mm Natural hemp
- Four ¼" Blue Chevron beads
- Watch face with bars, Watch buckle

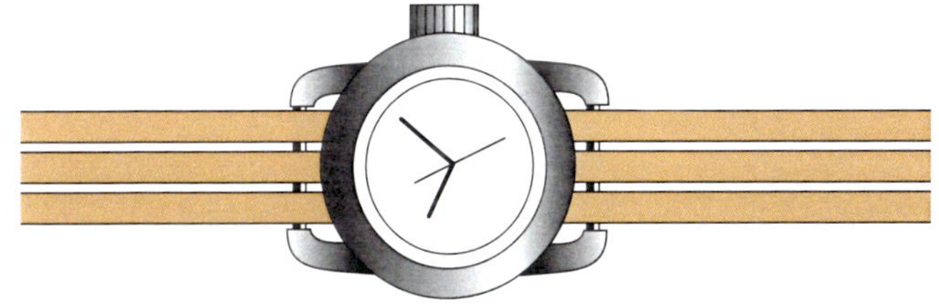

1. Fold 72" cords in half; mount to watch buckle with Lark's Head Knots, two on one side of tongue and 2 on the other side. Using the 2 outside cords from each side as one, tie 10 Square Knots over the 4 center cords.

2. Separate cords into 2 groups of 4 cords. Tie one Square Knot with each group. Using the 3 outside cords from each group, tie 6 Half Knot Twists with each group. Add a bead to the 2 inside cords not used in the twist.

3. Repeat Step 2.

4. Separate the cords into 2 groups of 4 cords, tie one Square Knot with each group. Thread cords between the bar and watch face, under the watch face, and out between the watch face and bar on the other side. Repeat Step 2 twice. Separate the cords into 2 groups of 4 cords, tie one Square Knot with each group.

5. Using the 2 outside cords from each group as one, tie 2 Square Knots over the 4 center cords. Trim 2 of the center cords, dot cut ends with glue. Tie 8 Square Knots over the 2 remaining filler cords. (To make the band longer, add more Square Knots; to make it shorter, tie fewer Square Knots.) Pull the last knot very tight.

6. Finish End - Separate the cords into 3 groups of 2 cords each. Braid for 1½". Fold braid to back of band, glue in place for 1". Before glue is dry, make holes for buckle tongue by pushing the end of a large needle through the band between each Square Knot. Trim ends when glue is dry.

7. Band Holder - Braid three 6" cords for 1½". Circle this braid around the band about 1" from the buckle. Secure the ends to the back of the band with glue. Trim ends when glue is dry.

Basic Instructions for Bags

Begin at the top of bag - Center one 120" holding cord on knotting board; use T-pins to pin to sides of board. Bundle the long ends and pin aside. Mount one-half of the knotting cords onto the holding cord with the Lark's Head Knot Variation. Center one 40" piece of holding cord directly beneath first holding cord; pin to the left side of board. Hold the mounting cord in your hand as you knot.

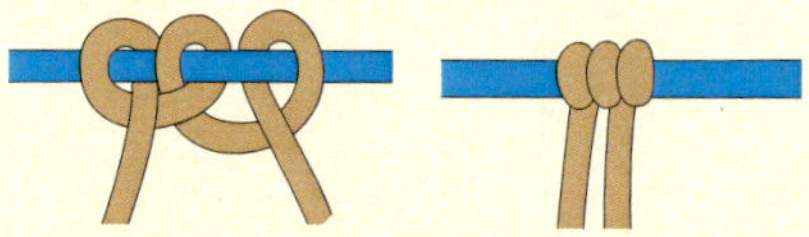

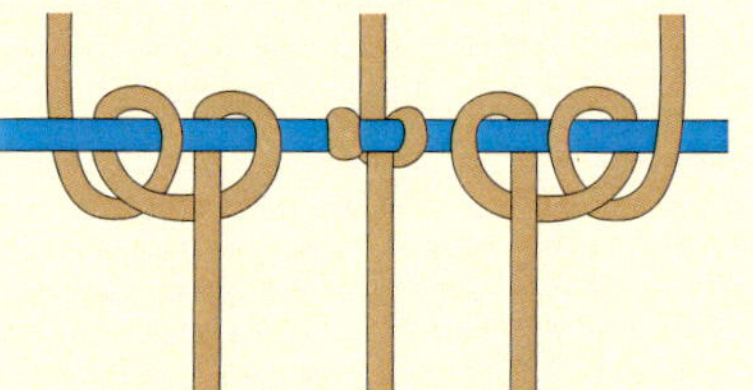

**Larks Head Mounting Variation
TO BEGIN THE BAG**

Tie one row of Horizontal Double Half Hitch Knots from left to right across the holding cord, pulling knots up against the row above. (On some bags, you will tie a second row of Horizontal Double Half Hitch. To do this, anchor the holding cord to the board with a pin, right next to the last knot, and work from right to left).

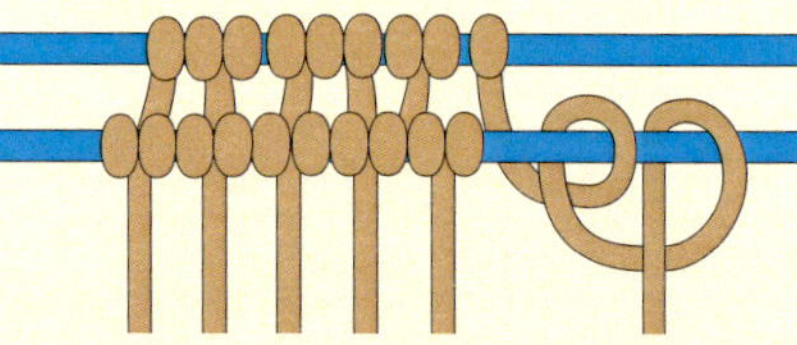

**Left to Right   Right to Left
Horizontal Double Half Hitch**

Body of bag - Begin tying Alternating Square Knot pattern, working from left to right. Follow individual instructions for the front of bag.

Bottom of bag - Pin one of the 16" holding cords to the left side of board, leaving a 6" tail. Tie 1 row of Horizontal Double Half Hitch Knots, left to right. Anchor the holding cord to

**Horizontal Double Half Hitch
ROW 1 - Left to Right**

Tiny Beginner Bag

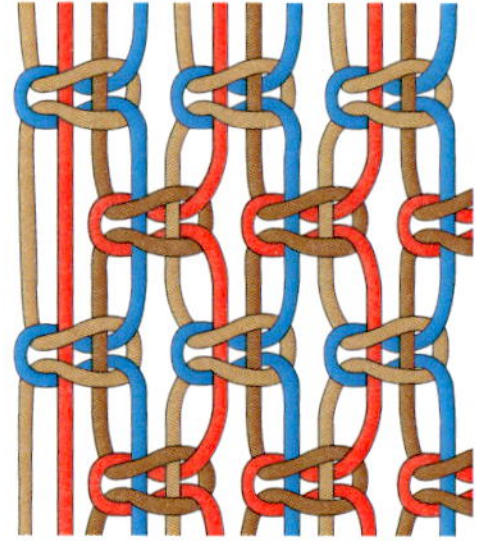

- Sixteen 20" pieces of 1mm hemp for body of bag
- Two 120" pieces of hemp for holding/neck cords
- Two 40" pieces of hemp for holding cords
- Two 10" pieces of hemp for holding/bottom cords
- Thirteen ¼" Ivory bone beads for necklace

1. Follow Basic Instructions to begin.

2. Tie the **Alternating Square Knot** pattern (page 14) for 2".

3. Tie 2 rows of Horizontal Half Hitch for bottom of bag.

4. Back of Bag - Knot same as the front.

5. Finish - Follow Basic Instructions to end.

6. Necklace - Half Hitch Twist and a bead every 1½".

Copper & Blue Amulet Bag

1mm HEMP: • Twenty-eight 25" pieces for body of bag • Two 120" pieces for holding/necklace cords • Two 40" pieces for holding cords • Two 16" pieces for holding/bottom cords

the board with a pin, right next to the last knot. Tie a second row, right to left, back across the holding cord.

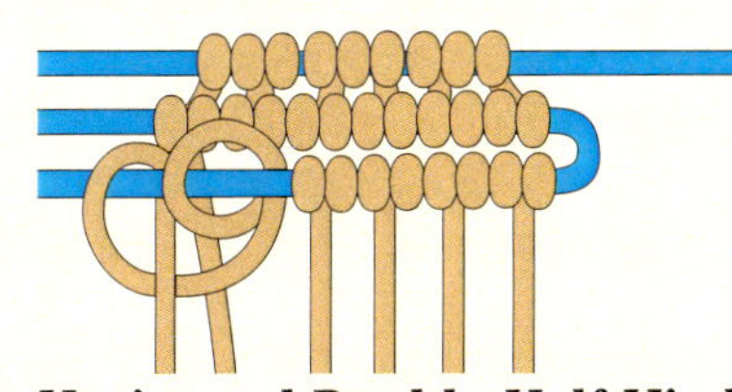

**Horizontal Double Half Hitch
ROW 2 - Right to Left**

Back of bags - Begin back of bag the same as the front, using the second half of the knotting cords, and the other 120" & 40" holding cords. The back of every bag is knotted in the Alternating Square Knot pattern (see page 14). Hold back up against front to see how many rows you need to make them the same length. Tie two rows of Horizontal Double Half Hitch Knots across the bottom, using the other 16" holding cord (see **Bottom of Bag,** above).

Fringe - If you **do not** want fringe: Before sewing sides together, use knotting cords at bottom of bag to tie front to back , on what will be the inside of bag. Dot knots with glue. Allow to dry, trim evenly.

If you **do** want fringe: Sew sides of bag together, leaving ends of knotting cords hanging free from bottom of bag. Tie a few cords together across bottom of bag to secure.

Finishing - Sew front to back using the "tails" of the holding cords; do not pull too tight. Knot ends of tails together at top, on the inside of bag. Trim the ends, or add to necklace filler cords for a few knots and trim out.

Necklace - At each side of the bag, you will have two long knotting cords (the 120" mounting cords) and two shorter filler cords (the 40" holding cords). Tie 3 Square Knots, then continue Square Knots, or Half Knot Twist. You can also leave spaces between knots, and add whatever beads you wish. For endings, see Closure, page 3.

BEADS: • Three 8mm Copper beads • Six ¼" Blue glass donut beads • Any desired beads for necklace

1. Follow Basic Instructions to begin.

2. Front of Bag - Tie 4 rows of Alternating Square Knot pattern.

3. Separate into 7 groups of 4 cords each. Working from left to right, tie 3 rows of Alternating Square Knot pattern with first two groups of cords. Tie 6 Half Knot Twists with 3 center groups. With the last 2 groups, tie the Alternating Square Knot pattern (page 14) for 3 rows.

4. Tie 2 rows of Alternating Square Knot pattern with all cords.

5. Again, separate into 7 groups of 4 cords each. Working from left to right, tie 6 Half Knot Twists with 1st, 3rd, 5th, & 7th groups. Add 1 Blue bead, 1 Copper bead, 1 Blue bead to 2nd, 4th, 6th groups.

6. Tie 2 rows of Alternating Square Knot pattern with all cords.

7. Tie 2 rows of Horizontal Half Hitch for bottom of bag.

8. Back of bag and finishing - follow Basic Instructions using Alternating Double Square Knot pattern.

9. Necklace - Knot necklace with Square Knots, add beads as desired.

Fringed Bag with Clasp

MATERIALS:

1mm HEMP: • Twenty-four 28" pieces for body of bag • Two 120" pieces for holding cords • Two 40" pieces for holding cords at top of bag • Four 16" pieces for holding cords at top and bottom of bag • Two 30" pieces for clasp-strap knotting cords • Two 15" pieces for clasp-strap filler cords

BEADS: • Forty ⅜" Red horn tube beads • One 1" Red horn tube bead for clasp; six more for necklace, if desired

1. Front of Bag - Follow Basic Instructions to begin. Tie a 3rd row of Horizontal Half Hitch, using the same holding cord.

2. Starting at one side, add 1 tube bead to each pair of cords across (12 beads). Using one 16" piece of holding cord, tie 2 additional rows of Horizontal Half Hitch under beads.

3. Tie 3 rows of Alternating Square Knot.

Using the sixth cord in from the edge on each side, thread cords horizonally through each end of a 1" Red tube bead (to act as a clasp). The bead will have one cord going into and one cord coming out of each end. Pin cords and bead up out of the way.

Tie the fourth row as usual. For the next row, unpin and return cords to their groups. Tie pattern as usual. Do not pull cords coming out of bead too tight. Tie 3 more rows (a total of 8 rows).

4. Bottom of Bag - follow Basic Instructions.

5. Back of Bag - follow Basic Instructions.

6. Clasp-Strap - Find the center of the two 30" cords. Loop cords (from inside to outside) around the center Square Knot on the back of bag, 5 rows down. Tie Square Knots for 4"; tie a Bauble Knot. Tie two more Square Knots. Tie 2 Overhand Knots, one on top of the other. Trim ends.

7. Finish - Follow Basic Instructions to complete bag. For fringe, add tube beads randomly to 2 cords at a time. Secure beads with Overhand Knots. Trim ends.

8. Necklace - Square Knots with a bead every 2" along the necklace.

Yellow & Black Beeper Bag "The Beeper Keeper"

MATERIALS:

1mm HEMP: • Twenty-eight 28" pieces for body of bag • Two 120" pieces for holding/neck cords • Two 40" pieces for holding cords • One 10" piece for holding cord • Two 16" pieces for holding cords at bottom of bag

BEADS: • Three 1" Yellow and Black horn beads • Nine ¼" Black horn bicone beads • Any desired beads for necklace portion

1. Front of Bag - Follow Basic Instructions to begin. Tie 3rd row of Horizontal Half Hitch using 10" holding cord. (This cord will be knotted into the necklace for a few inches, then cut off).

2. Tie 3 rows of Alternating Square Knots. On the next row, tie Alternating Square Knot pattern, adding a Black bead in place of the first and last knots.

Separate into 7 groups of 4 cords each. With first and last 2 groups, tie Alternating Square Knot pattern for 5 rows, adding a Black bead in place of center knot on every other row. Add a Yellow and Black bead to each of the 3 center groups.

3. Tie one row of Alternating Square Knots, but add a Black bead in place of the first, middle and last knot of the row. Tie one row of Alternating Square Knots.

4. Bottom of Bag - Follow Basic Instructions.

5. Back of Bag - Follow Basic Instructions.

6. Finish - Follow Basic Instructions to complete the bag.

7. Necklace - Leave a 2" space, 1 Square Knot, add bead, 1 Square Knot. Repeat.

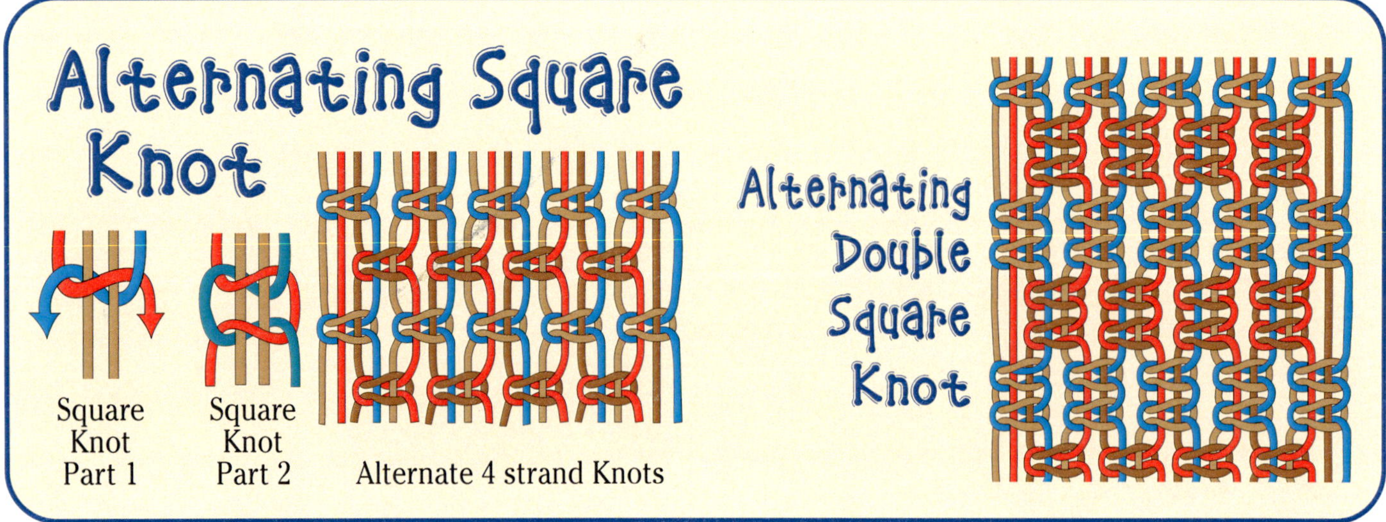

Beaded Fringe Bag

MATERIALS:

1mm HEMP: • Twenty-four 25" pieces for body of bag • Two 120" pieces for holding/neck cords • Two 40" pieces for additional holding cords at top of bag • Two 16" pieces for holding cords at bottom of bag

BEADS: • Five ¼" Red/Blue chevron beads • Eighty-four Orange E beads • Forty-four ¼" Blue glass donut beads • Any desired beads for necklace

1. Front of Bag - Follow Basic Instructions to begin.

2. Tie 5 rows of Alternating Square Knot pattern.

Add an Orange bead to every cord. Tie one row of the Alternating Square Knot pattern.

3. For the next row of Square Knots, add a chevron bead onto all 4 cords in place of the knot (5 beads).

Tie one row of Alternating Square Knot pattern.

4. Bottom of Bag - Follow Basic Instructions.

5. Back of Bag - Follow Basic Instructions.

6. Finish - Follow Basic Instructions to complete the bag. For fringe, add two Blue beads, 2 Orange beads, 2 Blue beads onto 2 cords. Secure beads with an Overhand Knot. Continue across bottom of bag. Trim ends.

7. Necklace - Half Hitch Twist with 2 Blue beads at 1" and 2" intervals.

Large White Beaded Cross

MATERIALS:
1mm HEMP:
• 80" piece for upright knotting cord
• 20" piece for upright filler/bead carrier cord
• Two 120" pieces for crosspiece/necklace knotting cords
• Two 18" pieces for crosspiece filler cord
BEADS: • Seven 8mm bone melon beads
• Five 1" bone hair pipe beads

NOTE: Tie all knots very snugly. Knotting begins at the **bottom** of the cross.

1. To Make the Upright - Center a melon bead on one 80" and one 20" cord. Tie the first half of a Square Knot. Pin to a knotting board.

2. Pin or keep one filler cord (now the bead carrier cord) out of the way. Tie the second half of the Square Knot over the other filler cord; tie 6 more Square Knots. Add a tube bead to bead carrier cord that was set aside.

Tie the first half of a Square Knot over filler and bead carrier cord, keeping the bead on top of knotting.

3. Again, pin bead carrier cord out of the way. Tie the second half of the Square Knot; tie 6 more Square Knots. Add a tube bead to bead carrier cord.

Tie the first half of a Square Knot over filler and bead carrier cords, keeping the bead on top of knotting; then add a melon bead to the bead carrier cord. Tie Second half of Square Knot over both cords.

4. Arms of the Cross - Repeat Steps 1 and 2 using one 120" cord and one 18" cord. Repeat for other arm.

5. Join arms to Upright - Pin one arm to each side of the upright. Bring all cords except the upright knotting cords together. Use the upright knotting cords to tie the first half of a Square Knot over all other cords.

Pin the bead carrier cord out of the way. Tie the second half of the Square Knot; tie 6 more Square Knots, then add a tube bead to the bead carrier cord. Tie the first half of a Square Knot over all cords. Add a melon bead to the bead carrier cord; and tie the second half of the Square Knot.

6. Finish the Necklace - Separate the cords into 2 groups of 6 cords. Each group should contain 2 long knotting cords and 4 shorter filler cords.

On each side of necklace: Tie 2 Square Knots, cut out two short filler cords, dot the cut ends with glue. Tie one Square Knot. Add a melon bead to all cords. Tie Square Knots for 12".

7. Finish Ends - At one end, tie 2 Overhand Knots, one on top of the other. On the other end of the necklace, tie an Overhand Knot leaving a ¾" space for a loop. Trim the ends. Stiffen back of cross with glue.

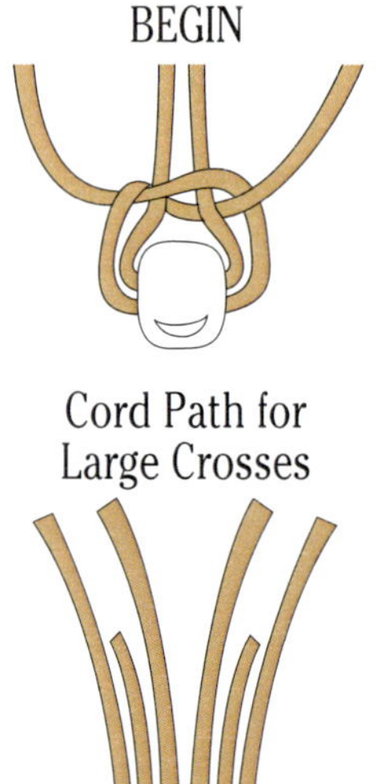

Yellow & Black Beaded Cross

MATERIALS:
1mm HEMP:
• 60" piece for upright knotting cord
• 15" piece for upright filler/bead carrier cord
• Two 110" pieces for crosspiece/necklace knotting cords
• Two 15" pieces for crosspiece filler cord
BEADS: • Five ½" Yellow/Black tube beads
• 9 small Black glass donut beads
• Two ¼" Black bicone beads

NOTE: Tie all knots very snugly. Knotting begins at the **bottom** of the cross.

1. To Make the Upright - Center three Black glass beads on one 60" and one 15" cord. Tie the first half of a Square Knot. Pin to a knotting board.

2. Pin or keep one filler cord (now the bead carrier cord) out of the way. Tie the second half of the Square Knot over the other filler cord; tie 3 more Square Knots. Add a tube bead to bead carrier cord that was set aside.

Tie the first half of a Square Knot over filler and bead carrier cord, keeping the bead on top of knotting.

3. Again, pin bead carrier cord out of the way. Tie the second half of the Square Knot; tie 3 more Square Knots. Add a tube bead to bead carrier cord.

Tie the first half of a Square Knot over filler and bead carrier cords, keeping the bead on top of knotting; then add Black bicone bead to the bead carrier cord. Tie Second half of Square Knot over both cords.

4. Arms of the Cross - Repeat Steps 1 and 2 using one 110" cord and one 15" cord. Repeat for other arm.

5. Join arms to Upright - Pin one arm to each side of the upright. Bring all cords except the upright knotting cords together. Use the upright knotting cords to tie the first half of a Square Knot over all other cords.

Pin the bead carrier cord out of the way. Tie the second half of the Square Knot; tie 3 more Square Knots, then add a tube bead to the bead carrier cord. Tie the first half of a Square Knot over all cords. Add Black bicone bead to the bead carrier cord; and tie the second half of the Square Knot.

6. Finish the Necklace - Separate the cords into 2 groups of 6 cords. Each group should contain 2 long knotting cords and 4 shorter filler cords.

On each side of necklace: Tie 2 Square Knots, cut out two short filler cords, dot the cut ends with glue. Tie Square Knots for 12".

7. Finish Ends - At one end, tie 2 Overhand Knots, one on top of the other. On the other end of the necklace, tie an Overhand Knot leaving a ¾" space for a loop. Trim the ends. Stiffen back of cross with glue.

Knotted Crosses

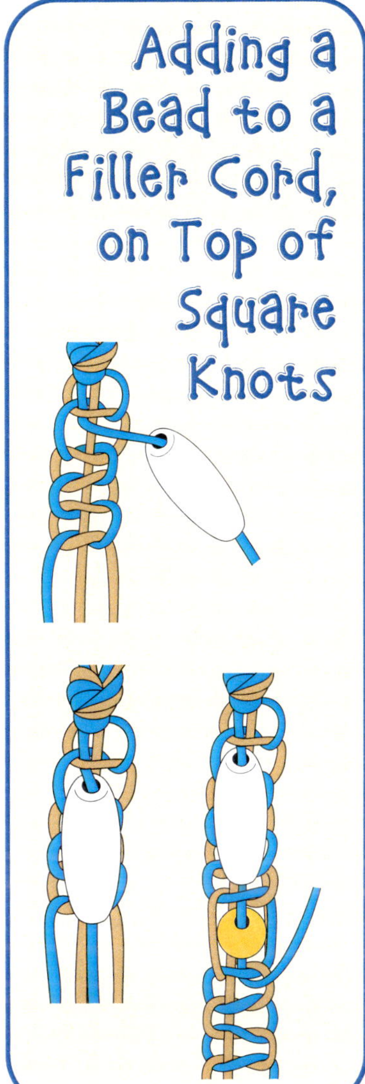

Create
Crosses
for Hemp
Necklaces
and Chokers

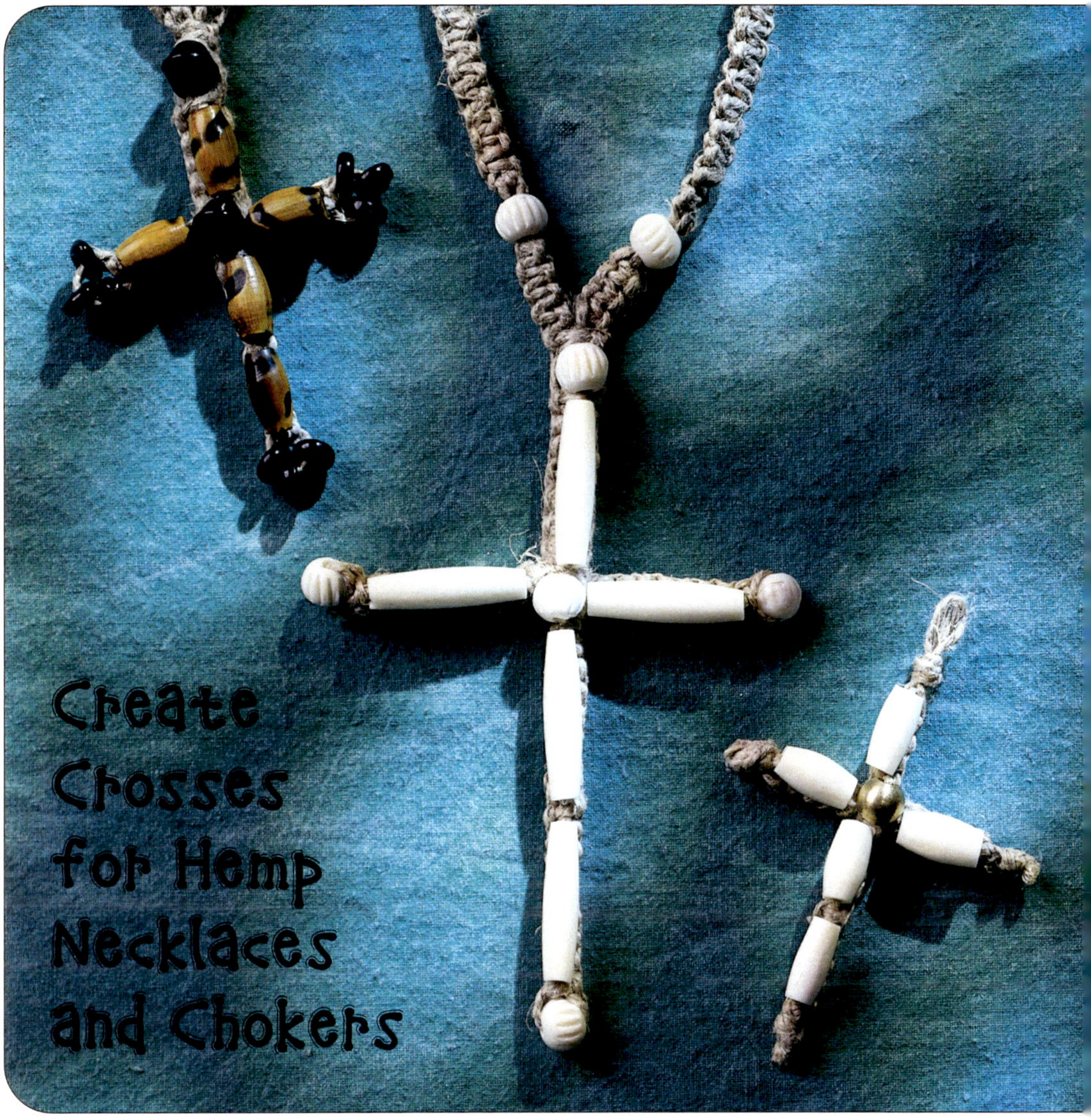

Small White Hanging Cross with a Gold Bead

MATERIALS:
NOTE: Begin at the **top** of the cross and work down.
1mm HEMP: • One 30" piece for upright knotting cords • One 15" piece for upright filler cords • Two 20" pieces for arm knotting cords • Two 14" pieces for arm filler cords
BEADS: • Five ½" Ivory tube beads • 8mm brass bead

1. Make the Upright - Fold one 30" and one 15" cord in half. Tie an Overhand Knot, leaving a ¾" loop to hang the cross from a bracelet or necklace.

2. Tie the first half of a Square Knot over 2 cords. Pin one filler cord aside: this is now the bead carrier cord. Tie the second half of the Square Knot over 1 cord. Tie 3 more Square Knots (over 1 cord). Add an Ivory tube bead to bead carrier cord. Tie the first half of a Square Knot over 2 cords; add a Gold bead to the bead carrier cord. Tie the second half of the Square Knot.

3. Arms of the Cross - For each arm, fold one 20" cord in half; tie an Overhand Knot at fold. Repeat Step 2 for each arm.

4. Join Arms to Upright - Pin one arm to each side of the upright. Bring all cords except the upright knotting cords together. Use the upright knotting cords to tie the first half of a Square Knot over all other cords.

5. Pin the bead carrier cord out of the way. Tie the second half of the Square Knot; tie 3 more Square Knots, then add a tube bead to the bead carrier cord. Tie the first half of a Square Knot over 4 cords. Pin bead carrier aside; tie the second half of the Square Knot; tie 3 more Square Knots. Add an Ivory tube bead. Tie an Overhand Knot with all cords. Trim the ends.

BEGIN

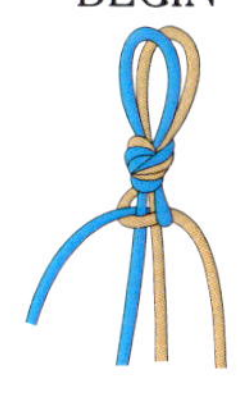

Cord Path for Small Cross

Begin at the **top** and work down.

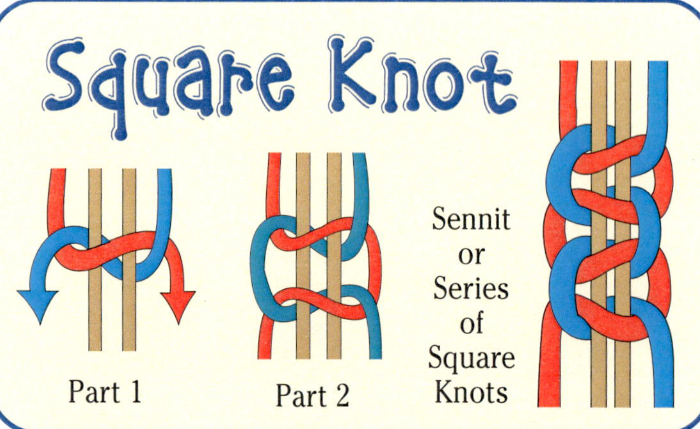

Square Knot
Part 1
Part 2
Sennit
or
Series
of
Square
Knots